Candlemaking
for the first time®

Candlemaking
for the first time®

Vanessa-Ann

Sterling Publishing Co., Inc.
New York

Chapelle Ltd.

Owner: Jo Packham

Editor: Karmen Quinney

Staff: Areta Bingham, Kass Burchett, Jill Dahlberg,
Marilyn Goff, Holly Hollingsworth, Susan Jorgensen,
Barbara Milburn, Linda Orton, Cindy Stoeckl,
Sara Toliver, Kristi Torsak, Desirée Wybrow

Graphic Artist: Kim Taylor

Photography: Kevin Dilley for Hazen Photography

Special Thanks

We would like to offer our sincere appreciation for
the valuable support given in this ever-changing
industry of new ideas, concepts, designs, and
products. Several projects shown in this publication
were created with outstanding and innovative
products developed by Yaley Enterprises,
7664 Avianca Drive, Redding, CA 96002
website: www.yaley.com

Library of Congress Cataloging-in-Publication Data

Candlemaking for the first time / Vanessa-Ann.
    p. cm.
    "A Sterling/Chapelle book."
    Includes index.
    ISBN 0-8069-7196-7
    1. Candlemaking. I. Vanessa-Ann Collection (Firm)

TT896.5 C365 2001
745.593'32--dc21   2001040082

15 16 17 18 19 20

Published in paperback 2004 by
Sterling Publishing Co., Inc.
387 Park Avenue South, New York, NY 10016
© 2001 by Chapelle Limited
Distributed in Canada by Sterling Publishing
℅ Canadian Manda Group,165 Dufferin Street,
Toronto,Ontario, Canada M6K 3H6
Distributed in the United Kingdom by GMC Distribution Services,
Castle Place,166 High Street, Lewes, East Sussex, England BN7 1XU
Distributed in Australia by Capricorn Link (Australia) Pty Ltd.
P.O. Box 704, Windsor, NSW 2756, Australia

Printed in China
All Rights Reserved

Sterling ISBN 0-8069-7196-7 (hardcover)
                1-4027-1352-5 (paperback)

For information about custom editions, special sales, premium and
corporate purchases, please contact Sterling Special Sales
Department at 800-805-5489 or specialsales@sterlingpub.com.

My candle burns at both ends; it will not last the night; but ah, my foes, and oh, my friends—it gives a lovely light.

Edna St. Vincent Millay
A Few Figs from Thistles

Table of Contents

Candlemaking for the first time
8

Candlemaking for the first time

Introduction

Candles are more than just a source of light. For centuries they have been used for symbolic and religious purposes. Candles also serve as a focal point for celebrations throughout the world.

The first candles, tallow candles, were made from beef or mutton fat. These candles produced black smoke and a rancid smell. Beeswax offered a more decorative and better smelling candle. However, with the cost of beeswax being so high, only the rich or clergy could purchase these higher quality candles. Eventually, the development of paraffin and stearin increased the availability of decorative and scented candles. Through the centuries, the materials needed to create candles have advanced, while the method of creating a candle has stayed the same.

Although candles are no longer a necessity for light, their popularity is enormous. They are still used for symbolic and religious reasons. However, the use of candles in today's society has a much broader spectrum. Candles are a very versatile item. Some offer healing and relaxation through their scent. Others contain a scent that repels mosquitoes. The variety of colors and shapes in which they are available adds to their simple and timeless beauty. Candles can add a unique touch to any type of setting. Their flickering light seems to draw people together. The look of a room can be enhanced simply by the way a candle is used.

Candlemaking can produce so many unique results. With *Candlemaking for the first time* as a guide, candles such as molded, double mold, container, dipped, rolled, and gel candles can be made by almost anyone. Learn to decorate the candles you have made, using decoupaging and painting techniques.

Page after page will offer fun and elegant ways to embellish the candles you have made. Discover contemporary ideas for decorating with candles to create a relaxed and intimate atmosphere.

Creating the finished projects shown in this book may take some time and practice, since this is your first time candlemaking. However, once the nine basic techniques of candlemaking are mastered, the possibilities of creating scent, beauty, and light are endless.

How to use this book

For the person who is candlemaking for the first time, this book provides a comprehensive guide to supplies, tools, and techniques that can be used to create fabulous decorative and functional candles.

Section 1: Candlemaking Basics familiarizes you with the basic tools and supplies you need to begin.

Section 2: Techniques contains instructions for nine projects that can be made using basic candlemaking techniques. Each technique builds on that which was learned in the previous technique from making a simple molded candle to a candle that has been dyed and scented to look like a country apple.

Section 3: Projects Beyond the Basics expands on the techniques learned in Section 2 with twenty-one additional projects that are a bit more complex and sometimes combine two or more techniques.

Section 4: Decorating with Candles features the fabulous effects that can be achieved through the candlemaking and decorating with the candles.

The purpose of *Candlemaking for the first time* is to provide a starting point and to teach basic skills. The more you practice candlemaking, the more comfortable you will feel. Allow yourself a reasonable amount of time to complete your first project—remember this is your first time. You will soon discover that the techniques are easy to master.

After you have completed the first few projects, you will be surprised by how quickly you will be able to finish the remaining projects. Take pride in the talents you are developing and the unique designs only you can create.

You can't light a candle to show others the way, without feeling the warmth of that bright little ray . . .
Unknown

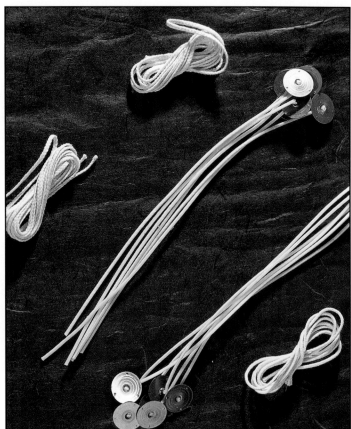

Section 1: *candlemaking basics*

What do I need to get started?

To begin candlemaking, all you need to do is take a trip to the local craft store or candle-making supplier to find a wide array of supplies. You probably already have many of the supplies around the house.

The following list of tools and supplies is necessary for creating candles. In addition, each technique or project gives a list of other items needed for that specific project.

Candle Dye Chips—used to dye the melted wax.

Candle Molds—used to mold candles into desired shapes and sizes.

Candle Scents—used to scent the melted wax.

Candle Thermometer—used to determine the precise temperature of wax.

Containers (not shown)—used to contain soft waxes while burning.

Craft Scissors—used to trim soft candle wax and wicks.

Double Boiler—used for melting wax. Make certain water does not boil dry. *Note: There are a few different options to choose from, depending on the amount of wax being melted. A container such as a coffee can or large soup can on a small rack inside of a saucepan filled with water can be easily substituted for a double boiler.*

Hammer & Screwdriver—used to break wax into smaller pieces.

Heating Element (not shown)—used to melt wax. Use either a stove or hot plate.

Kitchen Scale—used to weigh wax.

Large Plastic Trash Bag (not shown)—used to prevent scattering chips while breaking up wax.

Liquid Measuring Cups (not shown)—used to measure liquid ingredients.

Measuring Spoons—used to measure ingredients, following manufacturer's instructions.

Metal Pouring Pot—used to contain and pour molten wax.

Metal Spoons—used to mix dyes and scents into melted wax. Use a separate spoon for each dye color.

Mold Release (not shown)—used to coat the inside of molds for easy candle removal. Vegetable oil can be easily substituted.

Mold Sealer—used to secure wick and seal wick holes in molds.

Paper Towels (not shown)—used to wipe melted wax from equipment while still warm.

Paring Knife (not shown)—used to cut soft cold wax and trim candles.

Pencils—used to hold wick in place while creating candles.

Primed Wicks—used to burn candles. These wicks have been chemically treated.

Tape Measure—used to measure candle and wick dimensions.

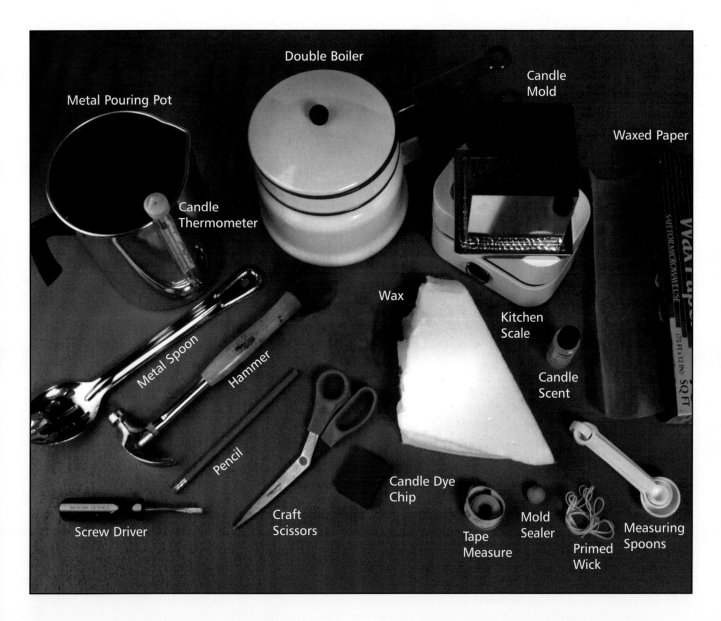

Metal Pouring Pot

Double Boiler

Candle Mold

Waxed Paper

Candle Thermometer

Metal Spoon

Hammer

Wax

Kitchen Scale

Candle Scent

Pencil

Screw Driver

Craft Scissors

Candle Dye Chip

Tape Measure

Mold Sealer

Primed Wick

Measuring Spoons

Waxed Paper—used to cover and protect work surface.

Waxes—used to create a candle. There are several types of wax used for candlemaking: bead, beeswax, gel, blended paraffin, and paraffin.

What safety precautions should I know before starting?

The following precautions are strongly recommended for your safety. When working with melted wax, it is a good idea to have baking soda and a fire extinguisher handy. Wax can be volatile and may ignite without warning. Please review the following items:

• Never use water to put out a wax fire. Smother the fire with baking soda.

• Use the lid to your double boiler to smother a wax fire.

• Never leave melting wax unattended. Always be aware of the wax's flash-point temperature. Keep a thermometer in the melting wax so you can be certain of the temperature.

• Never allow wax temperature to exceed 280°F.

• Always keep children and pets away from hot wax.

• Never allow wax to drip onto heating element. It may ignite upon contact and could cause a fire.

• Never store wax anywhere near heat. Always store wax in a cool dry location.

• Avoid heating wax in a microwave. It will collect energy from the inside out and can bubble, explode, or catch fire.

• Use only fragrances and dyes designed specifically for candlemaking.

• Be aware of aluminum molds when they contain hot wax. The aluminum molds get very hot and can burn your skin.

• Always pour wax with a container that can withstand high temperatures, and that has a spout and a handle.

• If melted wax comes in contact with skin, bathe the area immediately in cold water. Peel off the wax and treat burned area as any other burn or scald.

• Do not allow water to drip into melted wax as it will burst and could burn the skin.

• Never pour melted wax down the drain.

What do I need to know about waxes?

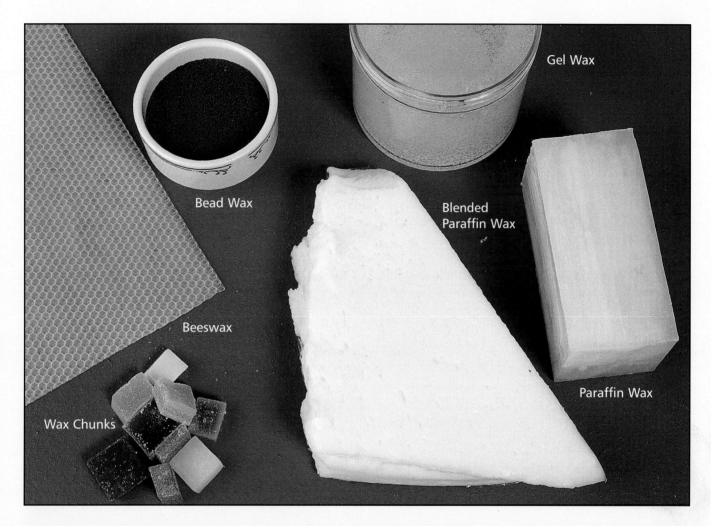

Gel Wax

Bead Wax

Blended Paraffin Wax

Beeswax

Paraffin Wax

Wax Chunks

The most essential ingredient in a candle is wax. The type of wax used, amount of wax used, and the temperature of melted wax will effect the final look of the candle.

Waxes used to create the candles in this book include:

Bead Wax—is wax that has been granulated into small beads. It can be found in a variety of colors and scents.

Beeswax—comes in blocks or sheets. It can be natural, unbleached, or bleached white. It offers a natural honey fragrance. When added to paraffin wax, it will help to lengthen the burn time.

Blended Paraffin & Paraffin Waxes—are petroleum-based waxes. Paraffin wax can be used plain, or it can come in a variety of blends to be used in creating specific candles.

Gel Wax—is a clear gel that can be purchased at your local craft store. We have also provided the ingredients and instructions for making gel wax in the Basic Gel Candle on pages 46–47.

Wax Chunks—come in a variety of colors. They can be melted down when small portions of wax are needed. They can also be embedded into a candle for a unique look.

How much wax do I need to use?

Calculate amount of wax needed (for the mold, container, or desired height of dipped candle) by filling the mold/container with water and measuring it—3 ounces of cold wax are needed for every 3½ fluid ounces of water.

How do I melt wax?

Melted wax can be volatile. Prepare and use caution and safety measures when handling wax. Please refer to What safety precautions should I know before starting? on page 14 before melting wax.

1. Place the block of paraffin wax into a large plastic bag, then place on a solid surface. Using hammer and screwdriver, break wax into small pieces that will fit into top of double boiler. *Note: Softer waxes can be cut with a paring knife.*

2. Make certain top section of double boiler is deep enough to accommodate length of thermometer so bulb does not touch bottom of pan. Separate top and bottom sections of double boiler. Place wax pieces into top of double boiler.

3. Fill bottom section of double boiler with water. Replace top section. Make certain water does not boil dry.

4. Set double boiler on heating element and bring water to boiling point. The wax will begin to melt, becoming a clear liquid.

5. Place thermometer in melting wax and reduce heat to medium low. If water begins to boil rapidly, reduce heat to a gentle boil to prevent water from splashing into wax container. Make certain heat is not reduced too much, as doing so will cause difficulty in keeping the temperature accurate.

6. Once wax is melted and is at the specified temperature, add stearin if necessary, dye, and scent. This may lower the temperature. Make certain wax is brought back up to temperature required.

How do I pour melted wax?

This book recommends that the melted wax be poured from the double boiler into a pouring pot. Using a pouring pot reduces the chance of spilling melted wax and makes filling molds or containers easier and safer. A pouring pot is not necessary when pouring large amounts of wax into another large container or when conciseness is not an issue.

Once the melted wax has reached the required temperature for candle, remove top section of double boiler from bottom section. Be aware of steam, and water dripping from bottom of top section. Carefully pour melted wax into pouring pot. Do not fill pouring pot more than 70 percent full. Replace top section.

When pouring melted wax, make certain of the following items:

• When filling a candle mold, candle container, or topping off a candle, make certain to use a pouring pot.

• Always pour melted wax carefully and slowly.

• Clean up all wax spills immediately.

• Wipe off all wax drippings on sides of double boiler or pouring pot immediately.

What candlemaking additives can I use?

Sometimes when you purchase paraffin wax you will need to add hardeners or other additives to keep it from being damaged by the sun or to make it opaque. Here is a list of some additives and their purposes.

Luster Crystals—provide a brilliant sheen and opaqueness and a longer burning candle. Recommended use per two pounds of wax is one teaspoon. Luster crystals must be melted first then added to your melted wax.

Microcrystalline Wax—makes candle wax harder. Recommended use per pound of wax is two tablespoons. It must be melted first, then added to melted wax as it will not melt in the wax by itself.

Snow Wax—makes the candle wax opaque with a high luster. It also prevents hot-weather sag, increases the burning time, and improves the surface texture. Recommended use per pound of wax is one teaspoon. It is recommended that Snow wax be melted separately.

Stearin—improves the candle's burning time and gives an opaque or white appearance. Recommended use per pound of wax is two tablespoons.

Vybar—makes the candle harder and cuts down on wax shrinkage. Recommended use per pound of wax is two teaspoons. Start with one teaspoon per pound then add more if necessary. It will also cause your candle to be opaque. Do not use more than the recommended amount.

What do I need to know about candle dyes?

Dyes for candlemaking come in several forms: chip, flake, liquid, and powder. They all come in a broad range of colors. Colors can also be mixed and matched for endless possibilities. This book uses the dye-chip form because it is readily available and easy to use.

Candle Dye Tips:

• Be careful when using candle dye. Clothes and some plastic equipment can become permanently stained.

• Too much dye can affect the candle's burning qualities.

• Too much heat can cause discoloration, at time of heating or within a short time after.

• Avoid using clear wax when making a black candle. Use pieces of scrap wax, then add needed amounts of black.

What do I need to know about candle scents?

Scents for candlemaking come in several forms: liquid, natural herbs, and solid-wax perfume chips. They all come in a broad range of scents. This book uses the liquid form because it is readily available and easy to use.

Candle Scent Tips:

• Add candle scent just before pouring to keep evaporation to a minimum.

• Avoid adding too much scent as this may cause mottling or pitting, making removal of candle from mold difficult.

What do I need to know about wicks?

Wicks are what helps the candle burn. Wicks must be carefully chosen to ensure proper burning. Primed wicks are made of braided cotton and specially treated to slow the burning rate. The three basic wicks used in this book are flat-braided, square-braided, and wire-core. Pretabbed wicks are available in these basic types. The tab on a wick is used to anchor the wick to the bottom of the container.

Flat-braided Wicks—used for dipped taper candles.

Square-braided Wicks—used for square or round pillar candles.

Wire-core Wicks—used for container candles and votives. This type of wick has a metal wire center, allowing the wick to stand upright in melted wax.

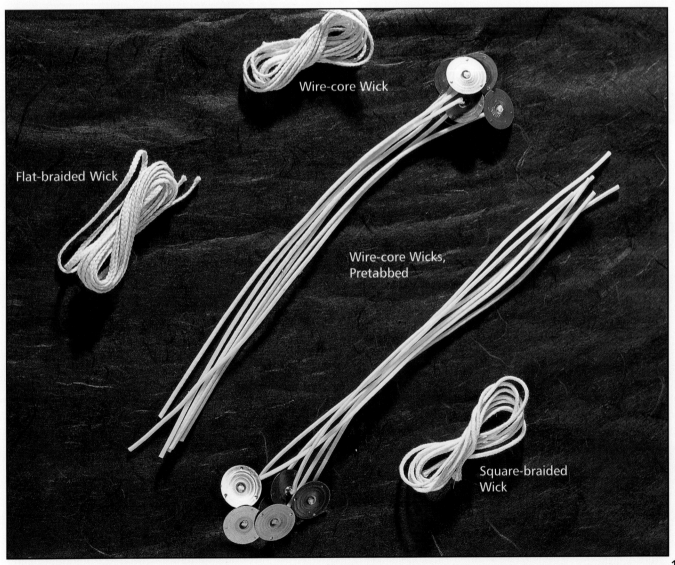

Wire-core Wick

Flat-braided Wick

Wire-core Wicks, Pretabbed

Square-braided Wick

How do I prime a wick?

Wicks can be purchased primed or unprimed. Prime an unprimed wick, using the following method:

1. Soak wick in melted wax for five minutes.

2. Remove saturated wick from melted wax and lay straight on waxed paper. Allow to harden.

How do I determine the size and length of wick needed?

Wick Size
The size of wick depends upon the diameter of the candle being made. Determine necessary size of wick, using the following method:

1. Using tape measure, measure diameter of mold, container, or desired thickness of dipped candle.

For candles with a burn area up to 2" in diameter, use small-sized wicks. For candles 2"–3", use medium-sized wicks. For candles 3"–4", use large-sized wicks.

Wick Length
In some cases, you may wish to leave a longer wick that can be knotted or embellished with beads and charms for a more decorative effect or for gift giving. Determine necessary length of wick, using the following method:

1. Using tape measure, measure height of mold, container, or desired height of dipped candle.

2. Add 2" to that measurement.

3. Cut length of wick to new measurement.

What do I need to know about molds?

Candle molds can be purchased at your local craft store or from candlemaking suppliers. Molds are available in an endless variety of shapes and sizes, from simple geometrics to ornate fruits and flowers. Molds are relatively inexpensive, and their sturdiness allows for long-lasting, repeated use. They are made from acrylic, metal, plastic, or rubber.

Many household cartons and containers make excellent molds. Anything that can be peeled, pulled, or broken off from a finished candle works well. However, in this book we will be using candle molds.

How do I know what temperatures are required for different types of molds?

Acrylic molds	180°–210°F
Clay molds	180°–210°F
Glass molds	170°–200°F
Metal molds	180°–210°F
Plaster molds	160°–180°F
Rubber molds	160°–180°F
Tear-away molds	160°F

How do I clean my candle molds?

Molds should always be kept clean in order to provide the best results. Candle molds should be clean and free from old candle wax before using. Do not scrape or scratch inside of molds when cleaning them, it will mar future candles. Candle molds can be cleaned using the following three methods:

Method 1
1. Fill sink with hot water and a small amount of liquid dish soap. Allow candle molds to soak for 15 minutes.

2. Wash candle molds, being careful of any sharp edges. Dry molds thoroughly. Dry seamless candle molds upside down on a cookie sheet covered with paper towels.

Method 2
1. Place candle molds on a cookie sheet covered with paper towels in a 200°F oven for 7–8 minutes. The paper towel will absorb the melted wax.

2. Wipe off any remaining wax from candle mold immediately.

Method 3
1. Use cleaner designed for metal molds, following manufacturer's instructions.

How do I prepare my work space?

Setting up your work space properly will make a large difference in the final results of your candles. We recommend that you work in the kitchen for ease and convenience. The following items are needed to prepare your work space: heating element, paper towels, pot holder (optional), and waxed paper.

1. Cover any surface that you will be working on with waxed paper. This will protect your work space and allow spilled wax to be reused.

2. Place additional sheets of waxed paper underneath candle molds and containers. Make certain that all items are within your reach.

3. Never allow wax to drip onto heating element. It may ignite upon contact and could cause a fire.

How do I clean up after I am finished?

Candle cleaning kits can be purchased to aid in removing stubborn stains and wax buildup from equipment and supplies. Following are a few methods to help in cleanup after candlemaking:

• Pour excess wax into an old pan lined with waxed paper. Never pour wax down the drain. It will cool and clog the drain. Unused wax can be melted and reused.

• Place supplies such as molds and metal spoons in boiling water until wax melts. Using tongs, remove items from water. Using paper towels, wipe items clean.

• Discard old metal soup and coffee cans, and other replaceable equipment.

• Place glass items in freezer. Wax will shrink and easily pop out.

How do I troubleshoot in candlemaking?

When learning a new craft, mistakes and problems will occur. However, certain problems tend to be more common among certain types of candles. Most of these problems can be corrected through practice and knowing what went wrong. Following are troubleshooting ideas in candlemaking:

Candle burning straight down the middle
• A candle made from a hard wax will burn straight down the wick, leaving the sides of the candle unmelted. The crater created will make it difficult for the flame to sustain itself. A softer wax, such as a container wax, could be used. However, using a wax with a lower melting point may create a pool of melted wax around the base of a pillar candle.

• A small, similarly scented votive or tea light could be placed in the cavity.

Candle color changes
• Wax was too hot when color was added. Avoid heating wax above 190°F that will be colored.

• Candle was exposed to direct sunlight. Many colors fade in sunlight. UV-protective additives are available.

Candle stops burning
• Additives such as color, spices, or essential oils of inferior quality can clog the wick.

Candle will not burn
• Wick was not primed. Saturate the wick with liquid wax or light it upside down to allow melted wax to prime wick.

Candle will not release from mold
• Make certain to always coat the mold with a mold release.

- A high percentage of beeswax may produce a candle that is sticky or does not shrink enough for easy release. Beeswax is less than ideal for using in molded candles.

- Place candle and mold into freezer or refrigerator for 5–10 minutes. Remove and check to see if candle releases.

- Candle may be run under hot water for release, although this may cause imperfections on the candle surface.

- Check molds for pits or dents.

Candles leaving excess wax on container walls
- Container candles burn best when they are lit for a minimum of four hours at a time. Burning a candle for short periods of time will cause unburned wax on container walls.

- Use a container wax or a wax with a lower burning point.

- Use a larger wick size.

Candle cracks
- Candle was cooled too fast.

- Candle was left in freezer too long.

Candle drips
- Wick is too small, it may not be able to absorb and burn the amount of wax melting around it.

- Wick is the wrong type for the wax blend.

- Wick is not properly centered. Check the position of the wick after candle is out and manually center it, if possible.

- Wax used was too soft and has too low of a melting point.

- Check for a draft around the flame.

Outside of candle looks old or dusty
- Polish the outside of the candle with a nylon stocking or almond oil.

- Overdip candle to renew its look.

Candle has pits and bubbles
- Wax was too cold when poured.

- Wax was poured too fast.

- Mold release was applied too heavily.

- Mold should be clean and dust-free before pouring wax.

Scent in candle is not strong enough
- Allow candle to burn one hour before judging strength of scent, because scent primarily rises from the liquid wax pool.

- Rubbing hands over the outside of a candle should activate scent in a candle that has lost fragrance on the outer surface.

Shrink wells
- This is a normal occurrence in paraffin wax blends. As wax cools, an indentation will form around the wick. Remelt remaining wax and fill to the top of indentation, making certain that wick is still centered. Try not to pour wax over the top, as this will set a line in candle. Allow wax to set. Repour wax as needed for an even candle.

- Occasionally, the shrink well comes at the bottom of the candle. You can straighten the bottom of the candle by trimming it off or melting it flat on a frying pan lined with aluminum foil.

Sides of candle cave in
• Air bubbles may be trapped inside candle. This problem can be prevented by tapping mold or perforating with a skewer around the wick to eliminate bubbles after pouring candle.

Smoking candle
• Wick is too thick.

• Wick is the wrong type for the wax blend.

• Wick is too long. Trim wick to ¼".

• Check for drafts around the flame.

Sputtering flame
• Wick is drawing from an air or oil pocket that has formed in the candle. This problem can be prevented by tapping mold or perforating with a skewer around the wick to eliminate bubbles after pouring candle.

• Pouring from a wet container may allow water to drop inside wax and form a water pocket.

Unintentional mottling or snowflake pattern
• Wax was too cold when poured.

• Candle was cooled too slowly.

• Too much stearin was added.

Weak flame or drowning wick
• Wick is too small.

• Wick is too loose in the candle.

• Melting point of the wax is too high for the size of wick used.

How do I care for finished candles?

• Keep lighted candles out of reach from children and pets.

• Never leave candles unattended.

• Store candles in a cool, dry, dark place. Make certain they are placed flat in a drawer or box to prevent warping.

• Clean dusty or dirty tapers or pillars by wiping them with a nylon stocking. If candles seem a bit dry, wipe them with a small amount of vegetable oil.

• Avoid exposing candle to direct sunlight or artificial light for an extended period of time.

• Refrigerate or freeze candles before using them to make them burn slowly and evenly.

• Carve away enough wax with a sharp paring knife to expose the fresh wick if a wick becomes too short to light. Shave ¼" of the wax from the top of the candle so the wick will be exposed to the air. Gently shape and smooth the cut edges of the candle with the heat of another flame.

• Extinguish candles that are smoking or have burned down to within 2" of the holder.

• Fit candles snugly into holders. Candles that are too lose or too tight may tip over.

• Extinguish candles with a candle snuffer or by blowing gently.

Section 2: *techniques*

1
technique

What You Need to Get Started:

Candle thermometer
Craft scissors
Double boiler
Empty soup can
Metal pouring pot
Mold: pillar
Mold release
Mold sealer
Mold-blend paraffin wax (1 lb)
Pencil
Primed wick: square-braided

How do I make a candle using a candle mold?

Candles can be molded into a variety of shapes and sizes. Today's molds are made from a variety of different materials, each type offering certain advantages and disadvantages. This basic molded candle was created with a pillar mold for a simple yet elegant look.

Basic Molded Candle
Photograph on page 27.

Here's How:

1. Prepare work space. Refer to How do I prepare my work space? on page 22.

2. Melt wax in double boiler until it reaches 194°–198°F. Refer to How do I melt wax? on page 16. Proceed with Steps 3–4 while wax is melting.

3. Cut appropriate sized wick to length. Refer to How do I determine the size and length of wick needed? on page 20.

4. Prepare mold, using the following technique:

a. Lightly coat inside of mold with mold release.

b. Thread wick through hole in bottom of mold.

c. Cover hole and secure end of wick on outside of mold with mold sealer to prevent any leaking that may occur when the wax is poured.

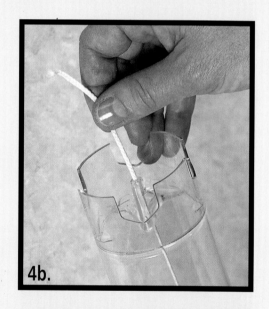
4b.

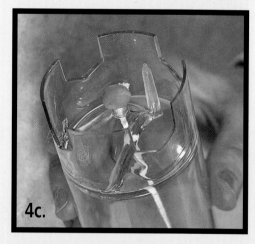
4c.

d. Tie opposite end of wick around a pencil. Place pencil on top rim of mold. Make certain that wick is centered and taut. If wick is not taut, tighten wick around pencil.

4d.

5. Using pouring pot, pour melted wax into the mold until mold is 90 percent full. Refer to How do I pour melted wax? on page 17. Allow wax to set. Make certain to set aside a small amount of that particular wax in empty soup can to top off the candle.

5

6. As wax cools, an indentation will form around the wick. Top off candle, using the following technique:

a. Remelt remaining wax and fill to the top of indentation, making certain that wick is still centered. Try not to pour wax over the top, as this will set a line in candle. Allow wax to set.

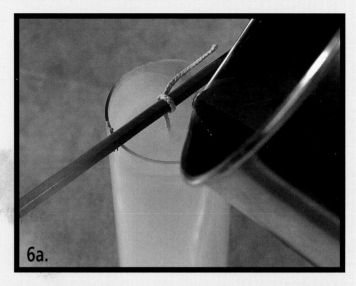

6a.

b. Repour wax as needed for an even candle. Allow wax to set.

7. Remove candle from mold, using the following technique:

a. Remove pencil. Remove mold sealer. Tip mold upside down. Candle should slide out on its own. If it does not work, place mold with candle in freezer for 5–10 minutes. Remove from freezer. Tip mold upside down. Candle should slide out on its own.

8. Trim wick at top of candle to ¼". Trim wick at bottom of candle flush with base.

2 technique

How do I make a candle a different color using dye?

Wax can be dyed in a wide spectrum of colors from intense jewel tones to light cream satin. If colored candles are left in direct sunlight, they will begin to fade. This summer blue candle was made by using a medium blue dye chip.

What You Need to Get Started:

Candle dye chip:
  med. blue
Candle
  thermometer
Craft scissors
Double boiler
Empty soup can
Metal pouring pot
Metal spoon
Mold: pillar
Mold release
Mold sealer
Pencil
Pillar-blend paraffin
  wax (1 lb)
Primed wick:
  square-braided

Basic Dyed Candle

Here's How:
1. Prepare work space. Refer to How do I prepare my work space? on page 22.

2. Melt wax in double boiler until it reaches 190°F. Refer to How do I melt wax? on page 16. Proceed with Steps 3–4 while wax is melting.

3. Cut appropriate sized wick to length. Refer to How do I determine the size and length of wick needed? on page 20.

4. Prepare mold. Refer to Technique 1, Step 4 on pages 28–29.

5. Dye wax, using the following technique:

a. Add one dye chip to melted wax. Mix well.

5a.

6. Using pouring pot, pour melted wax into the mold until mold is 90 percent full. Refer to How do I pour melted wax? on page 17. Allow wax to set. Make certain to set aside a small amount of that particular wax in empty soup can to top off the candle.

7. Top off candle. Refer to Technique 1, Step 6 on page 29.

8. Remove candle from mold and trim wick. Refer to Technique 1, Steps 7–8 on page 29.

3
technique

What You Need to Get Started:

Candle dye chip:
  ivory
Candle scent:
  vanilla
Candle
  thermometer
Craft scissors
Double boiler
Empty soup can
Metal pouring pot
Metal spoon
Mold: round pillar,
  1½" x 9½"
Mold release
Mold sealer
Pencil
Pillar-blend paraffin
  wax (1 lb)
Primed wick:
  square-braided

How do I make a candle fragrant using a scent?

Candles offer more than just light. A scented candle has the ability to set the mood, create an atmosphere, and evoke memories. With just one whiff of this vanilla candle, we can be transported to our childhood and a favorite famous French vanilla dessert.

Basic Scented Candle

Here's How:

1. Prepare work space. Refer to How do I prepare my work space? on page 22.

2. Melt wax in double boiler until it reaches 194°–198°F. Refer to How do I melt wax? on page 16. Proceed with Steps 3–4 while wax is melting.

3. Cut appropriate sized wick to length. Refer to How do I determine the size and length of wick needed? on page 20.

4. Prepare mold. Refer to Technique 1, Step 4 on pages 28–29.

5. Dye wax. Refer Technique 2, Step 5 on page 30.

6. Scent wax, using the following technique:

a. Add 1–3 drops of candle scent to melted wax. Mix well. *Note: Fragrance is added last to keep evaporation to a minimum.*

6a.

7. Using pouring pot, pour melted wax into the mold until mold is 90 percent full. Refer to How do I pour melted wax? on page 17. Allow wax to set. Make certain to set aside a small amount of that particular wax in empty soup can to top off the candle.

8. Top off candle. Refer to Technique 1, Step 6 on page 29.

9. Remove candle from mold and trim wick. Refer to Technique 1, Steps 7–8 on page 29.

4
technique

What You Need to Get Started:

Candle dye chip:
  pale green
Candle scent:
  apple
Candle
  thermometer
Craft scissors
Double boiler
Empty soup can
Metal pouring pot
Metal spoon
Mold: two-piece,
  apple
Mold release
Mold sealer
Mold-blend par-
  affin wax
  (1 lb)
Primed wick:
  square-braided

How do I use a two-piece candle mold?

Two-piece molds offer a whole new variety of candles that can be created. They are easy to use. A ball mold can be used to create a billiard ball, a baseball or an orange. Just remember to secure the mold pieces tightly together.

Country Apple

Here's How:

1. Prepare work space. Refer to How do I prepare my work space? on page 22.

2. Melt wax in double boiler until it reaches 180ºF. Refer to How do I melt wax? on page 16. Proceed with Steps 3–4 while wax is melting.

3. Cut appropriate sized wick to length. Refer to How do I determine the size and length of wick needed? on page 20.

4. Separate mold pieces. Prepare two-sided mold, using the following technique:

a. Lightly coat inside of mold with mold release.

b. Thread wick up through hole in bottom piece of mold.

c. Thread wick up through hole in top piece of mold. Attach mold pieces tightly together.

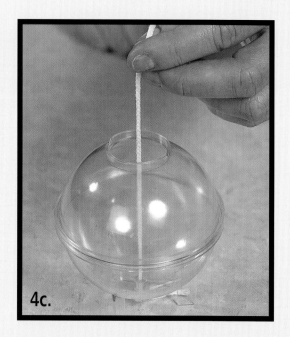

4c.

d. Cover hole and secure end of wick on outside of mold with mold sealer to prevent any leaking that may occur when the wax is poured.

e. Tie opposite end of wick around the rod that is included with two-piece mold. Place rod in grooves at top of mold. Make certain that wick is centered and taut. If wick is not taut, tighten wick around rod.

5. Dye wax. Refer to Technique 2, Step 5 on page 30.

6. Scent wax. Refer to Technique 3, Step 6 on page 32.

7. Using pouring pot, pour melted wax into the mold until mold is full. Refer to How do I pour melted wax? on page 17. Allow wax to set. Make certain to set aside a small amount of that particular wax in empty soup can to top off the candle.

8. Top off candle. Refer to Technique 1, Step 6 on page 29.

9. Remove candle from mold by separating mold pieces. Remove candle.

10. Trim wick. Refer to Technique 1, Step 8 on page 29.

Two-piece Candle Tip:
Two-piece candle molds can oftentimes leave seam lines on the candle. These lines can be easily removed. Holding a paring knife at a right angle on candle seam, turn candle until the entire seam is removed. Buff with a nylon stocking.

5
technique

Candle dye chip: purple
Candle scent: lilac
Candle thermometer
Container: glass
Container-blend paraffin wax (1 lb)
Craft scissors
Double boiler
Empty soup can
Metal pouring pot
Metal spoon
Primed wick: pre-tabbed, wire-core
Wick sticker

How do I make a candle using a container?

An alternative to making a candle in a mold is making one in a decorative container that will house the candle. Container candles are attractive, functional, and versatile. The glass containers on the facing page have found a new life as candle containers. Make certain that the container can withstand the pouring temperature of the melted wax.

Basic Container Candle

Here's How:
1. Prepare work space. Refer to How do I prepare my work space? on page 22.

2. Melt wax in double boiler until it reaches 160°–165°F. Refer to How do I melt wax? on page 16. Proceed with Step 3 while wax is melting.

3. Cut appropriate sized wick to length. Refer to How do I determine the size and length of wick needed? on page 20.

4. Dye wax. Refer to Technique 2, Step 5 on page 30.

5. Scent wax. Refer to Technique 3, Step 6 on page 32.

6. Apply wick sticker to bottom of wick tab, then to inside bottom center of clean container.

7. Tie opposite end of wick around a pencil. Place pencil on top rim of mold. Make certain that wick is centered and taut. If wick is not taut, tighten wick around pencil.

8. Using pouring pot, pour melted wax into the container until container is 90 percent full. Refer to How do I pour melted wax? on page 17. Allow wax to set. Make certain to set aside a small amount of that particular wax in empty soup can to top off the candle.

9. Top off candle. Refer to Technique 1, Step 6 on page 29.

10. Trim wick at top of candle to ¼".

6 technique

How do I make a candle using the dipped method?

What You Need to Get Started:

Candle dye chip:
   blue
Candle scent:
   blueberry
Candle
   thermometer
Craft scissors
Dipping vat: 5" x
   12"
Double boiler
Metal spoon
Pencil
Taper-blend
   paraffin wax
   (4 lb)
Wick: flat-braided

A dipped taper candle is made by repeatedly dipping a wick into melted wax. The longer the taper is, the more time it will need to cool in the dipping process. The dipped tapers featured on page 40 were dipped more than 30 times.

Basic Dipped Taper Candles
Photograph on page 40.

Here's How:
1. Prepare work space. Refer to How do I prepare my work space? on page 22.

2. Melt wax in double boiler until it reaches 158°F. Refer to How do I melt wax? on page 16.

3. Dye wax. Refer to Technique 2, Step 5 on page 30.

4. Scent wax. Refer to Technique 3, Step 6 on page 32.

5. Pour wax into dipping vat.

6. Make dipped candle, using the following technique:

a. Cut wick to desired height of candle times two plus 2". Center and drape wick over pencil. Hold wick in center. Dip two ends into melted wax, up to 1" from pencil. Wait for sixty seconds. Remove wick from wax, making certain that the two ends do not touch.

6a.

b. Hold candles over dipping vat and allow candles to harden. This takes only a few minutes. Repeat dipping. After 3–4 dippings, use fingers to straighten wicks and candles as necessary.

c. Continue, dipping a little shorter than previous dipping.

d. Trim drips from bottom of candle several times during dipping process.

e. Repeat dipping, hardening, and trimming until candles have reached desired thickness. *Note: To give candles a glossy top coat, increase heat to 180°F and dip one last time.* Hang candles and allow to set.

7. Trim wick in center to separate candles or leave candles connected for storing or displaying.

Dipped Taper Candle Tip:
For ease in the dipping process as candles become thicker, you may need to remove the pencil and continue dipping by hand. Make certain that fingertips do not touch the melted wax.

How do I make a candle using bead wax?

Bead wax is a fun and easy wax to create a candle. There is no melting of wax or thermometers to watch. Bead wax can be mixed or layered for a colorful candle. This elegant candle was created by spooning copper bead wax into a glass container.

What You Need to Get Started:

Bead wax: copper
Container: glass
Craft scissors
Metal spoon
Primed wick:
   pretabbed, wire-
   core
Wick sticker

Basic Bead Wax Candle
Photograph on page 42.

Here's How:
1. Prepare work space. Refer to How do I prepare my work space? on page 22.

2. Cut appropriate sized wick to length. Refer to How do I determine the size and length of wick needed? on page 20.

3. Apply wick sticker to bottom of wick tab, then to inside bottom center of clean container.

4. Spoon bead wax into container until full. Make certain to keep wick centered.

5. Trim wick at top of candle to ¼".

41

Bead Wax Candle Tip: As candle burns, a solid pool of wax will form around wick. More beads can be added at future lightings.

How do I make a candle using beeswax?

Rolled beeswax candles are easy to make. Simply roll a beeswax sheet around a wick. The beeswax sheets are imprinted with honeycomb design and offer a delicious, yet natural scent. These candles were made from colored beeswax sheets.

Basic Rolled Beeswax Candle
Photograph on page 44.

Here's How:
Note: Beeswax candles tend to develop a powdery residue. Remove residue by blowing the candle with a blow dryer.

1. Prepare work space. Refer to How do I prepare my work space? on page 22.

2. Place beeswax sheet on work surface. Using craft knife and ruler, cut beeswax sheet lengthwise into three equal sections approximately 2¾" wide.

3. Using craft scissors, cut wick ¾" longer than one short edge of sheet.

4. Using blow dryer, warm beeswax until it becomes soft and pliable.
Continued on page 45.

Beeswax sheet:
  8¼" x 16¾"
Blow dryer
Craft knife
Craft scissors
Primed wick:
  square-braided
Ruler

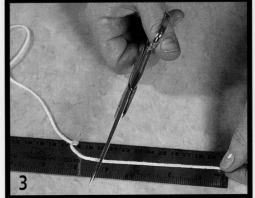

Continued from page 43.
5. Press wick into short edge, leaving ¾" length at one edge of beeswax. Begin rolling, making certain wick is firmly in place after the first roll.

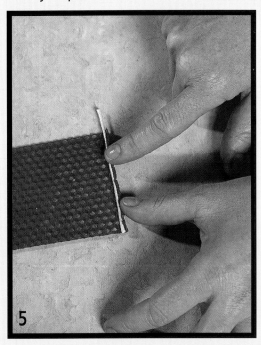

6. Continue rolling candle. *Note: The tighter the candle is rolled, the longer it will burn.*

7. When first section is completely rolled, place it on second section, with seams together, and continue rolling.

8. Repeat for remaining section.

9. When rolling is complete, press free edge into side of candle, smoothing in place with fingers.

10. Trim wick at top of candle to ¼".

9
technique

What You Need to Get Started:

Blow dryer
  (optional)
Candle scent: apple
Candle
  thermometer
Container: glass
Double boiler
Measuring cup
Measuring spoon
Metal pouring pot
Metal spoon
Mineral oil (16 oz)
Pencil
Primed wick: wire-
  core
Resin: CP9000
  (25 grams)

How do I make a candle using gel wax?

Gel wax can be made from scratch in your kitchen or it can be purchased. Whichever one you decide upon, the result will be the center of conversation, because of its transparency. Gel wax can be cubed, shredded, rolled, bubbly, or smooth. These candles appear as if the wick were floating in their contemporary containers.

Basic Gel Candle

Here's How:

1. Prepare work space. Refer to How do I prepare my work space? on page 22.

2. Using metal spoon, mix mineral oil and resin in double boiler. Allow to set at room temperature for one hour, stirring occasionally.

3. Melt resin mixture slowly, until it reaches 200°–210°F. Hold at this temperature for one hour or until gel is completely smooth like consistency of corn syrup. *Note: Never let the temperature of mixture exceed 230°F as the gel may scorch.*

4. Cut appropriate sized wick to length. Refer to How do I determine the size and length of wick needed? on page 20.

5. Scent wax. Refer to Technique 3, Step 6 on page 32.

6. Dip one end of wick into gel wax. Place wax-covered end in container and hold to bottom center, allowing wick to adhere to container.

6

7. Tie opposite end of wick around pencil. Place pencil on top rim of container. Make certain that wick is centered and taut. If wick is not taut, tighten wick around pencil.

8. Using pouring pot, pour melted gel wax into the mold until mold is 90 percent full. Refer to How do I pour melted wax? on page 17. Allow wax to set. *Note: If candle should shift or appears bumpy on top, use blow dryer to heat trouble area until flat.*

9. Remove pencil and trim wick at top of candle to ½".

Gel Wax Candle Tips:
Achieve a variety of effects using the following temperatures for gel wax:
180°–190°F lots of bubbles
190°–200°F fair amount bubbles
200°–210°F few to no bubbles

To ensure the gel wax is bubble free, heat container in a preheated oven at 150°F for 10 minutes before using.

Section 3: *projects beyond the basics*

1
project

What You Need to Get Started:

Candle dye chip: white
Candle scent: rose
Candle thermometer
Craft scissors
Double boiler
Empty soup can
Metal pouring pot
Metal spoon
Mold: large round
Mold release
Mold sealer
Pencils (3)
Pillar-blend paraffin wax (2 lb)
Primed wicks: pretabbed, square-braided (5)
Wick sticker

How do I create a candle with multiple wicks?

A multiwick candle is created by spacing several wicks equal distances apart. This multiwick candle contains five wicks. Think of the magic a candle flame provides to a room, then multiply this effect times five.

Multiple-wick Candle

Here's How:
1. Prepare work space. Refer to How do I prepare my work space? on page 22.

2. Melt wax in double boiler until it reaches 194°–198°F. Refer to How do I melt wax? on page 16. Proceed with Steps 3–6 while wax is melting.

3. Cut appropriate sized wicks to length. Refer to How do I determine the size and length of wick needed? on page 20.

4. Lightly coat inside of mold with mold release. Cover hole on outside of mold with mold sealer to prevent any leaking that may occur when the wax is poured.

5. Apply wick sticker to bottom of wick tabs. Apply first wick in center of mold. Apply remaining wicks evenly spaced between center wick and around outside edge of mold.

6. Tie opposite ends of wicks around pencils. Place pencils on top rim of mold. Make certain that wicks are straight and taut. If wicks are not taut, tighten wicks around pencils.

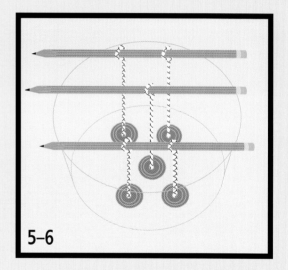

5–6

7. Dye wax. Refer to Technique 2, Step 5 on page 30.

8. Scent wax. Refer to Technique 3, Step 6 on page 32.

9. Make a multiple-wick candle. Refer to Technique 1, Steps 5–7 on page 29.

10. Trim wicks at top of candle to ¼".

2
project

What You Need to Get Started:

Candle dye chip: red
Candle scent: pomegranate
Candle thermometer
Craft scissors
Double boiler
Empty soup can
Measuring spoons
Metal pouring pot
Metal spoon
Mold: large heart
Mold release
Mold seal
Mold-blend paraffin wax (1 lb)
Pencil
Primed wick: square-braided
Snowflake oil (2½ tb)

How do I create a candle with snowflake effect?

Simply add snowflake oil to your melted wax to achieve a snowflake effect. The candle featured on the facing page with its snowflake blotches and spots of white would have been considered a mistake 20 years ago. It would have been remelted for another attempt. However, this type of candle is now considered chic.

Snowflake Candle

Here's How:

1. Prepare work space. Refer to How do I prepare my work space? on page 22.

2. Melt wax in double boiler until it reaches 194°–198°F. Refer to How do I melt wax? on page 16. Proceed with Steps 3–4 while wax is melting.

3. Cut appropriate sized wick to length. Refer to How do I determine the size and length of wick needed? on page 20.

4. Prepare mold. Refer to Technique 1, Step 4 on pages 28–29.

5. Add snowflake oil to wax. Mix well.

6. Dye wax. Refer to Technique 2, Step 5 on page 30.

7. Scent wax. Refer to Technique 3, Step 6 on page 32.

8. Make a heart-shaped candle. Refer to Technique 1, Steps 5–8 on page 29.

Snowflake Candle Tips:

The lesson to be learned from the origination of the snowflake design is that mistakes made during the candle-making process can oftentimes become a new technique.

It should also make you more willing to try something a little different than what the instructions state. After you have worked with the candlemaking process for awhile and are comfortable with the techniques, try changing the dyes, the amounts, or the sequence. The result may be a technique or design that is new and created by you.

3
project

Candle dye chips: green, ivory
Candle scent: apple
Candle thermometer
Craft scissors
Double boiler
Empty soup can
Metal cans (2)
Metal pouring pot
Metal spoon
Mold: 1" votive
Mold release
Mold sealer
Mold-blend paraffin wax (1 lb)
Pencil
Primed wick: square-braided

How do I make a multicolored layered candle?

A multicolored layered candle is made by pouring different colored waxes into the mold/container in layers. The number of colored layers depends on your own personal taste. Create a candle with several thin colored layers or a couple of thick layers as shown on the facing page.

Layered Candle

Here's How:

1. Prepare work space. Refer to How do I prepare my work space? on page 22.

2. Melt wax in double boiler until it reaches 194°–198°F. Refer to How do I melt wax? on page 16. Proceed with Steps 3–4 while wax is melting.

3. Cut appropriate sized wick to length. Refer to How do I determine the size and length of wick needed? on page 20.

4. Prepare mold. Refer to Technique 1, Step 4 on pages 28–29.

5. Divide and pour melted wax into two metal cans.

6. Dye wax a different color in each can. Refer to Technique 2, Step 5 on page 30.

7. Scent wax. Refer to Technique 3, Step 6 on page 32.

8. Using pouring pot, pour melted wax into the mold until mold is 50 percent full. Refer to How do I pour melted wax? on page 17. Allow wax to set.

9. Pour remaining color of melted wax into mold until 90 percent full. Allow wax to set. Make certain to set aside a small amount of that particular wax in empty soup can to top off the candle.

10. Top off candle. Refer to Technique 1, Step 6 on page 29.

11. Remove candle from mold and trim wick. Refer to Technique 1, Steps 7–8 on page 29.

4 project

What You Need to Get Started:

Candle dye: white
Candle scent: vanilla
Candle thermometer
Corrugated or ridged cardboard
Craft scissors
Double boiler
Duct tape
Empty soup can
Metal pouring pot
Metal spoon
Mold: square metal
Mold sealer
Mold-blend paraffin wax (1 lb)
Pencil
Primed wick: square-braided
Tape measure

How do I make an embossed candle?

A simple way to emboss a candle is to use corrugated cardboard. Corrugated cardboard comes in different-sized ridges and textures to fit your personal taste. The embossed candle on the facing page has a sleek contemporary look.

Corrugated Candle

Here's How:

1. Prepare work space. Refer to How do I prepare my work space? on page 22.

2. Melt wax in double boiler until it reaches 180°–199°F. Refer to How do I melt wax? on page 16. Proceed with Steps 3–6 while wax is melting.

3. Cut appropriate sized wick to length. Refer to How do I determine the size and length of wick needed? on page 20.

4. Lightly coat inside bottom of mold with mold release.

5. Using tape measure, measure height and circumference of mold. Using craft scissors, cut cardboard to these dimensions, making certain corrugated ridges are vertical. Trim edges where necessary to fit cardboard tightly inside mold. Tape long edges together on noncorrugated side, with corrugated side facing inward. Place cardboard into mold.

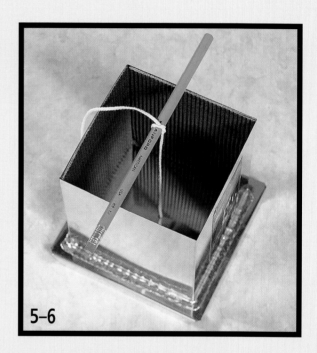

5–6

6. Prepare wick in mold. Refer to Technique 1, Step 4b–d on pages 28–29.

7. Dye wax. Refer to Technique 2, Step 5 on page 30.

8. Scent wax. Refer to Technique 3, Step 6 on page 32.

9. Using pouring pot, pour melted wax into the mold until mold is 90 percent full. Refer to How do I pour melted wax? on page 17. Allow wax to set. Make certain

56

to set aside a small amount of that particular wax in empty soup can to top off the candle.

10. Top off candle. Refer to Technique 1, Step 6 on page 29.

11. Remove pencil. Remove mold sealer. Using fingers, tap sides of mold. Pull cardboard from sides and remove from mold. If it does not work, place mold with candle in freezer for 5–10 minutes. Remove from freezer. Tip mold upside down. Candle should slide out on its own.

12. Using craft scissors, cut and peel cardboard from candle. *Note: The cardboard may leave layers of paper on the candle, giving the candle a textured look.*

13. Trim wick at top of candle to ¼". Trim wick at bottom of candle flush with base.

Corrugated Candle Tip:

If you do not want the textured look that the corrugated cardboard leaves on the candle, a rubber mold can be purchased that will give the embossed look without the paper.

5
project

What You Need to Get Started:

Candle
  thermometer
Craft scissors
Double boiler
Metal pouring
  pot
Metal spoon
Mold: tapered
  cup
Mold release
Mold seal
Mold-blend
  paraffin wax
  (1 lb)
Pencil
Primed wick:
  square-braided
Wax stars: clear
  (lg. bag)

How do I embed purchased wax shapes into a candle?

Wax shapes can be embedded in a candle by simply filling the mold with them and adding melted wax. This Star-filled Candle was created using clear wax stars and clear melted wax for a natural luminous effect.

Star-filled Candle

Here's How:

1. Prepare work space. Refer to How do I prepare my work space? on page 22.

2. Melt wax in double boiler until it reaches 194º–198ºF. Refer to How do I melt wax? on page 16. Proceed with Steps 3–5 while wax is melting.

3. Cut appropriate sized wick 4" longer than height of mold. Refer to How do I determine the size and length of wick needed? on page 20.

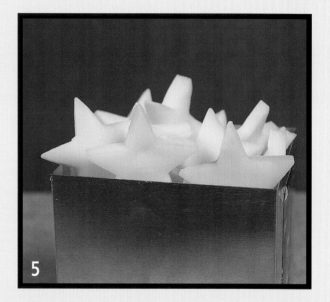

4. Prepare mold. Refer to Technique 1, Step 4 on pages 28–29.

5. Place wax stars as desired into mold from bottom to top, making certain wick remains centered. Make certain that many of the stars touch the side of the mold and extend above the mold.

6. Using pouring pot, pour melted wax into the mold until mold is 90 percent full. Refer to How Do I Pour Melted Wax? on page 17. Allow wax to set.

7. Remove candle from mold. Refer to Technique 1, Step 7 on page 29.

8. Trim wick at top of candle to 3". Trim wick at bottom of candle flush with base. *Note: Remember to trim wick to ¼" before burning.*

Wick Tip: Small ornaments or trinkets can be tied onto the end of wicks for a personal touch when giving your handmade candles away. Tell recipient to trim wick to ¼" before burning.

6
project

What You Need to Get Started:

Candle dye: olive
  green
Candle scent:
  eucalyptus
Candle
  thermometer
Container: shallow
  plastic 8" x 8"
Cookie cutters:
  round; star
Craft scissors
Double boiler
Empty soup can
Freezer
Metal can
Metal pouring
  pot
Metal spoon
Mold: square
  pillar
Mold release
Mold seal
Paper towels
Pencil
Pillar-blend par-
  affin wax (1 lb)
Primed wick:
  square-braided
Spatula

How do I embed just one or two wax shapes into a candle?

Embedding wax shapes in a candle takes a little more time and patience than a basic molded candle. However, the final result is worth it. These unique candles were created using the same technique, yet each has a look all its own.

Embedded Rustic Candle

Here's How:

1. Prepare work space. Refer to How do I prepare my work space? on page 22.

2. Melt wax in double boiler until it reaches 194°–198°F. Refer to How do I melt wax? on page 16. Proceed with Steps 3–5 while wax is melting.

3. Cut appropriate sized wick. Refer to How do I determine the size and length of wick needed? on page 20.

4. Prepare mold. Refer to Technique 1, Step 4a–c on page 28. Allow remaining portion of wick to hang over side of mold.

5. Place mold in freezer for 30 minutes. *Note: The reaction between the cool mold and the melted wax will cause a white film on the finished candle, creating a rustic look.*

6. Using pouring pot, pour wax to a depth of ½" into plastic container. Refer to How do I pour melted wax? on page 17. Allow wax to cool, but not set.

7. Using cookie cutters, cut entirely through layer of wax for one shape each. Do not remove.

8. Dye remaining wax in double boiler. Refer to Technique 2, Step 5 on page 30.

9. Scent wax. Refer to Technique 3, Step 6 on page 32.

10. Using spatula, remove shapes from container. Set aside.

11. Remove mold from freezer. Using paper towels, make certain to remove any traces of water in mold. *Note: If water drips into melted wax, it will pop and could burn the skin.*

12. Using pouring pot, pour melted wax into the mold until mold is 90 percent full. Wait 3–5 minutes until a thin film appears on surface.

13. Using paring knife, cut ½" in from edges around top of mold. Remove film from center and place film back in double boiler. Immediately pour remaining wax in the mold back into double boiler and remove from heat. *Note: This will leave a thin layer of wax on sides of mold.*

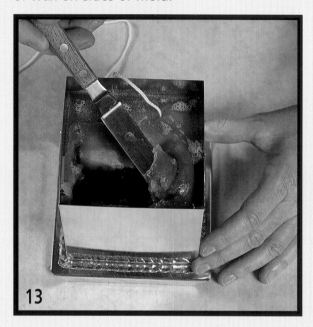

14. Using paper towels, clean off rim of mold.

15. Gently, press wax shapes into thin layer of wax around sides of mold as desired. Make certain to embed shapes into wax but do not break through thin wax layer.

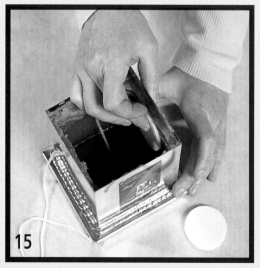

16. Tie remaining portion of wick around a pencil. Place pencil on top rim of mold. Make certain that wick is centered and taut. If wick is not taut, tighten wick around pencil.

17. Check temperature of melted wax in double boiler. Make certain it is 130°–140°F. Adjust as necessary.

18. Using pouring pot, pour melted wax into the mold until mold is 90 percent full. Make certain to set aside a small amount of that particular wax in empty soup can to top off the candle. Allow wax to set.

19. Top off candle. Refer to Technique 1, Step 6 on page 29. Repour wax as needed for an even candle. Allow wax to set.

20. Remove candle from mold and trim wick. Refer to Technique 1, Steps 7–8 on page 29.

How do I make a double-molded candle?

A double-molded candle is a shell of wax that holds a candle. As the candle burns down, the flame will light up the shell. Here, the golden glow of apples brings back memories of fall and hot apple cider.

Double-molded Candle

Photograph on page 64.

Here's How:

1. Prepare work space. Refer to How do I prepare my work space? on page 22.

2. Melt wax in double boiler until it reaches 165°–185°F. Refer to How do I melt wax? on page 16. Proceed with Step 3 while wax is melting.

3. Lightly coat inside of mold with mold release. Cover hole on outside of mold with mold sealer to prevent any leaking that may occur when the wax is poured.

4. Dye wax. Refer to Technique 2, Step 5 on page 30.

5. Scent wax. Refer to Technique 3, Step 6 on page 32.

6. Create candle mold. Refer to Project 6, Steps 12–14 on pages 61–62.

7. Gently, press some dried botanicals into thin layer of wax as desired. Make certain to embed into wax but do not break through thin wax layer.

8. Place pillar candle in center of mold.

9. Place remaining botanicals in mold.

10. Check temperature of melted wax in double boiler. Make certain it is 165°–185°F. Adjust as necessary.
Continued on page 64.

What You Need to Get Started:

Candle dye chip: gold
Candle scent: apple cinnamon
Candle thermometer
Craft knife
Double boiler
Dowel
Dried botanicals: cinnamon sticks; dried apples; dried berries; dried leaves
Empty soup can
Metal pouring pot
Metal spoon
Mold: large, rigid, round
Mold release
Mold seal
Mold-blend paraffin wax
Paper towels
Pillar candle: gold to fit inside of mold with 1" all around

Continued from page 63.

11. Using pouring pot, pour melted wax into the mold until mold is 90 percent full. Allow wax to cool, but not set. Make certain to set aside a small amount of that particular wax in empty soup can to top off the candle.

12. Using dowel, press down any items that may float to the top or out of place. Allow wax to set.

13. As wax cools, a cavity will develop around the top edge. Refer to Technique 1, Step 6 on page 29. Repour wax as needed for an even candle. Allow wax to set.

14. Remove candle from mold. Refer to Technique 1, Step 7 on page 29.

What kind of items can I embed in gel wax?

Any item that can withstand hot temperatures without melting can be placed in a gel wax candle. The possible trinkets and various containers that can be used to create a gel wax candle are endless. At a glance, the glass container featured on page 66 looks like it is simply holding a collection of seashells. But look again . . . it is a candle.

Seashell Gel Candle
Photograph on page 66.

Here's How:

1. Make gel wax. Refer to Technique 9, Steps 1–3 on page 47.

2. Cut appropriate sized wick to length. Refer to How do I determine the size and length of wick needed? on page 20.

3. Scent wax. Refer to Technique 3, Step 6 on page 32.

4. Prepare wick. Refer to Technique 9, Steps 6–7 on page 47.

5. Arrange seashells as desired in container. Make certain that wick is centered and taut. If wick is not taut, tighten wick around pencil.

6. Using pouring pot, pour melted gel wax into the container until container is 90 percent full. Refer to How do I pour melted wax? on page 17. Allow wax to set. *Note: If candle should shift or appears bumpy on top, use blow dryer to heat trouble area until flat.*

7. Remove pencil and trim wick at top of candle to ¼".

Embedded Gel Candle Tips:
Try embedding costume jewelry, dried botanicals, pennies, rocks, or marbles into a gel wax candle.

Several items along the same theme can be embedded into a gel candle.

What You Need to Get Started:

Blow dryer (optional)
Candle scent: lavender
Candle thermometer
Container: glass 10"
Double boiler
Measuring cup
Measuring spoon
Metal pouring pot
Metal spoon
Mineral oil (16 oz)
Pencil
Primed wick: flat-braided
Resin: CP9000 (25 grams)
Seashells: large bag

How do I make a scented oil lamp?

All that is needed for a scented oil lamp is a wick, a wick tube, lamp oil, and a glass container. For centuries, oil lamps were a necessity. Today, they are decorative functional centerpieces. The oil lamp featured on page 68 filled with realistic strawberries will compel your guests to take a second glance.

Blender Candle
Photograph on page 68.

Here's How:
1. Fill blender container with plastic strawberries. *Note: Make certain to tighten bottom of container.*

2. Insert wick into wick tube. Place wick tube in center of blender container, allowing it to extend above top of strawberries.

3. Fill blender container 90 percent full with lamp oil. This will cause strawberries to float.

4. Remove center piece from blender lid, then place lid onto blender.

5. Continue to fill blender container with lamp oil until oil reaches bottom of blender lid.

6. Adjust wick tube to show above lid.

7. Trim wick at top of wick tube to ¼".

Oil Lamp Tips:
Always place oil lamps in a secure area where they cannot be tipped over.

Oil lamps can be created using various containers and themes.

What You Need to Get Started:

Blender
Craft scissors
Lamp oil:
   strawberry
   scented (1 liter)
Plastic strawberries
   without stems
Wick: flat-braided
Wick tube: 6"

How do I make a candle tart?

Candle tarts are a wickless type of candle that are melted in a special container. They can be made in various shallow molds, muffin tins, and tart pans—hence the name "candle tart." The candle tarts featured on page 70 were made in tea-light candle molds and offer a lovely lavender scent.

Candle Tart

Photograph on page 70.

Here's How:

Note: Candle tarts can be made in various molds such as a metal petit four tin. Any type of tin can be used as long as it has a smooth surface with openings that are wider than the bases. This allows for easy melting.

1. Prepare work space. Refer to How do I prepare my work space? on page 22.

2. Melt wax in double boiler until it reaches 180°F. Refer to How do I melt wax? on page 16. Proceed with Step 3 while wax is melting.

3. Lightly coat inside of mold with mold release.

4. Dye wax. Refer to Technique 2, Step 5 on page 30.

5. Scent wax. Refer to Technique 3, Step 6 on page 32.

6. Sprinkle and stir dried lavender into melted wax.

7. Using pouring pot, pour melted wax into the mold until full to create candle tart. Refer to How do I pour melted wax? on page 17. Allow wax to set.

8. Remove candle tart from mold. Refer to Technique 1, Step 7 on page 29.

Candle Tart Tip:
Dye and scent candle tarts to match the occasion or upcoming season.

10 project

What You Need to Get Started:

Candle dye chip: white
Candle scent: lavender
Candle thermometer
Container-blend paraffin wax (1 lb)
Craft scissors
Double boiler
Dried lavender
Metal pouring pot
Metal spoon
Mold: tea-light
Mold release

How do I make a floating candle?

Floating candles are small candles with tops that are wider than their base—like a bowl. Floating candles, glittering in a container of water, are extremely attractive. However, they are even more stunning when incorporated into a theme as featured on page 72.

Floating Candle
Photograph on page 72.

Here's How:
1. Prepare work space. Refer to How do I prepare my work space? on page 22.

2. Melt wax in double boiler until it reaches 180°–194°F. Refer to How do I melt wax? on page 16. Proceed with Steps 3–4 while wax is melting.

3. Cut wick 1" higher than mold. Refer to How do I determine the size and length of wick needed? on page 20.

4. Lightly coat inside of mold with mold release.

5. Add stearin to melted wax. Mix well.

6. Dye wax. Refer to Technique 2, Step 5 on page 30.

7. Scent wax. Refer to Technique 3, Step 6 on page 32.

8. Using pouring pot, pour melted wax into the mold until full. Refer to How Do I Pour Melted Wax? on page 17. Allow wax to set.

9. Remove candle from mold. Refer to Technique 1, Step 7 on page 29.
Continued on page 72.

Floating Candle Tip:
Make certain that molds for floating candles are containers with openings wider than the bases. They can come individually or in sets of four or six.

What You Need to Get Started:

Candle dye chip: brown
Candle paint: gold metallic
Candle scent: pine
Candle thermometer
Craft scissors
Double boiler
Hot water
Metal pouring pot
Metal spoon
Mold: floating, pinecone
Mold release
Mold sealer
Mold-blend paraffin wax (1 lb)
Paintbrush: small
Primed wick: wire-core
Stearin (1 tb)
Wicking needle

Continued from page 71.
10. Dip wicking needle into hot water long enough to warm needle. Using wicking needle, pierce a hole through center of each candle. *Note: The hole should be a clean one, small enough to insert wick, but not large enough that wick slides out.* Immediately place wick through hole. The melted wax around the hole will seal the wick in place.

11. Using paintbrush, daub paint onto tips of pinecone candle.

12. Trim wick at top of candle to ¼".

How do I make candle garden stakes?

Candle garden stakes are molded candles with inserted wooden skewers. Highlight the party area with these tulip-shaped citronella candles. These candles will dissuade unwanted insects from joining the party, making it possible to enjoy the outdoors long after the sun has set.

What You Need to Get Started:

Candle dye chip: lt. green
Candle scent: citronella
Candle thermometer
Craft scissors
Double boiler
Hot water
Metal pouring pot
Metal spoon
Mold: tulip-shaped
Mold release
Mold sealer
Mold-blend paraffin wax (1 lb)
Primed wick: square-braided
Wicking needle
Wooden skewer

Citronella Candle
Photograph on page 74.

Here's How:
Note: Citronella candles are for outdoor use only.

1. Prepare work space. Refer to How do I prepare my work space? on page 22.

2. Melt wax in double boiler until it reaches 194°–198°F. Refer to How do I melt wax? on page 16. Proceed with Steps 3–4 while wax is melting.

3. Cut appropriate sized wick to length. Refer to How do I determine the size and length of wick needed? on page 20.

4. Lightly coat inside of mold with mold release. Cover hole with mold sealer to prevent any leaking that may occur when the wax is poured.

5. Dye wax. Refer to Technique 2, Step 5 on page 30.

6. Scent wax. Refer to Technique 3, Step 6 on page 32.

7. Using pouring pot, pour melted wax into the mold until mold is full. Refer to How do I pour melted wax? on page 17.

8. As wax cools, insert skewer ½" into center of candle. Allow wax to set.

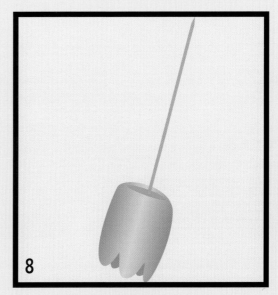

8

Continued on page 75.

Continued from page 73.

9. Remove candle from mold. Refer to Technique 1, Step 7 on page 29.

10. Dip wicking needle into hot water long enough to warm needle. Using wicking needle, pierce a hole through center of candle until it reaches skewer. *Note: The hole should be a clean one, small enough to insert wick, but not large enough that wick slides out.* Immediately insert wick. The melted wax around the hole will seal the wick in place.

11. Trim wick at top of candle to ¼".

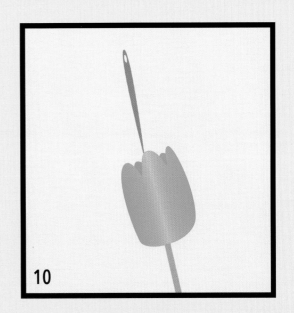

Citronella Candle Tips:

The wick of a citronella candle is typically larger to increase wax melting. The larger the pool of melted wax, the greater the scent and effectiveness. For best results, space candles every 5'–10'. If the weather is hot, moist, or windy, increase the number of candles. Place candles outdoors one hour before sunset. Candles are not effective until a pool of melted wax forms.

Citronella candles are most commonly poured into metal tins or galvanized buckets as shown on the right.

Citronella candles repel as many as 25,000 varieties of mosquitoes and are effective against some other small flying insects. However, some insects such as moths are attracted to the light of the flame.

13

project

What You Need to Get Started:

Baking sheets (2)
Candle dye chips:
  magenta; pink
Candle scent:
  cinnamon
Candle
  thermometer
Cookie cutter:
  heart
Craft scissors
Double boiler
Metal cans (2)
Metal pouring pot
Metal spoons (2)
Mold-blend par-
  affin wax
  (1 lb)
Pastry brush
Primed wick:
  square-braided
Spatula
Vegetable oil
Wick tab
Wicking needle

How do I make a stacked candle?

A stacked candle can be created in any desired shape. This stacked candle was created using a heart-shaped cookie cutter and a thin layer of wax. The thickness of the shapes depends on the depth of wax placed into the baking sheet. With all the possible shapes and colors, the fun will never end.

Stacked Heart Candle

Here's How:

1. Prepare work space. Refer to How do I prepare my work space? on page 22.

2. Melt wax in double boiler until it reaches 180°F. Refer to How do I melt wax? on page 16. Proceed with Step 3 while wax is melting.

3. Using pastry brush, brush baking sheets with vegetable oil.

4. Using pouring pot, divide and pour wax into two cans. Refer to How do I pour melted wax? on page 17.

5. Dye wax pink in one can and magenta in remaining can. Refer to Technique 2, Step 5 on page 30.

6. Scent wax in each container. Refer to Technique 3, Step 6 on page 32.

7. Pour one can of melted wax onto baking sheet to ¼" depth. Pour remaining can of melted wax onto remaining baking sheet.

8. Allow wax to cool, but not set. Using cookie cutter, cut entirely through layers of wax. Do not remove.

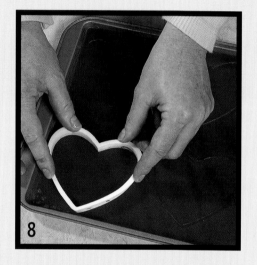

8

9. Using wicking needle, pierce a hole through center of each heart. Allow wax to set.

9

76

10. Using spatula, remove hearts from baking sheets.

11. Thread 12" length of wick onto wicking needle. Apply wick tab to one end of wick.

12. Using wicking needle, thread wick through heart holes. Stack hearts in color groups of three hearts, on top of each other.

Stacked Heart Candle Tip:
Stacked hearts are individually movable after assembly. Be careful when moving stacked hearts; because of their thinness, they are easily broken and/or chipped.

14 project

What You Need to Get Started:

Candle dye chip: yellow
Candle thermometer
Double boiler
Measuring spoons
Metal can
Metal fork
Metal spoon
Paraffin wax (1 lb)
Pillar candle: round, yellow
Spatula
Stearin (1 tb)

How do I use whipped wax?

Whipped wax can be used to create various decorative candles such as a snowball candle or an ice cream sundae candle. The candle featured on the facing page was covered with whipped wax to resemble a frosted cake.

Whipped Candle

Here's How:

1. Prepare work space. Refer to How do I prepare my work space? on page 22.

2. Melt wax in double boiler until it reaches 140°F. Refer to How do I melt wax? on page 16.

3. Add stearin to melted wax. Mix well.

4. Dye wax. Refer to Technique 2, Step 5 on page 30.

5. Pour melted wax into metal can. Allow wax to cool until a thin film appears on surface. *Note: The wax will first set on the top and around the sides and bottom of can.*

6. Using fork, whip wax until thick and foamy. *Note: This may take 5–10 minutes.*

7. Using spatula and working one area at a time, apply generous amount of whipped wax to candle. Continue until candle is covered. *Note: Whipped wax must be applied when warm. If wax cools too much, melt it down and begin again.*

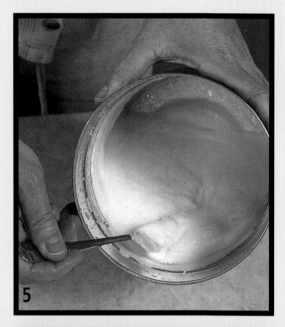

Whipped Candle Tip:
Candles also can be dipped into the whipped wax, using the following method:
Holding onto wick of candle, dip into whipped wax in one smooth motion.

15
project

What You Need to Get Started:

Candle thermometer
Cloth: soft
Craft scissors
Dipping vat: deep enough to accommodate enough wax to submerge candle
Double boiler
Gold leafing
Motifs: paper
Nylon stocking: soft
Paintbrush: soft
Paper towels
Paraffin wax (½ lb)
Permanent marker
Pillar candle: square, white
Water
Waxed paper

How do I use melted wax to decoupage a candle?

There are many ways to enhance the surface of a candle to create a more interesting appearance. The candle featured on the facing page has been decoupaged using melted wax and decorative paper, then gold leafing has been added for an extra touch of class.

Decoupaged Candle

Here's How:

Note: This method of decoupage should only be used with 3"-diameter candles or larger. Trim away sides as candle burns down.

1. Prepare work space. Refer to How do I prepare my work space? on page 22.

2. Trim motifs to fit candle.

3. Melt wax in double boiler until it reaches 194ºF. Refer to How do I melt wax? on page 16. Proceed with Step 4 while wax is melting.

4. Prepare dipping vat using the following technique:

a. Place candle in dipping vat and fill dipping vat with water until it covers the candle. Hold candle down, as it will float to the top. Remove candle.

b. Using permanent marker, mark water level on outside of dipping vat. Pour water out. Using paper towels, dry candle and dipping vat thoroughly.

5. Pour melted wax into dipping vat to 1" depth over mark on vat.

6. Holding onto wick of candle, dip entire candle into melted wax in one smooth motion. Remove and place candle on waxed paper.

7. Quickly adhere motifs onto candle. Smooth as needed. Holding onto wick, dip entire candle into melted wax in one smooth motion. Remove and place candle on waxed paper.

8. Allow wax to set. *Note: The candle will look cloudy when it comes out but will dry clear.*

9. Using paintbrush and a tapping motion, adhere gold leafing to remaining sides of candle. Adhere leafing around top edges of candle.

10. Using cloth, buff and distress leafing as desired.

11. Using nylon stocking, buff candle for a smooth, shiny finish.

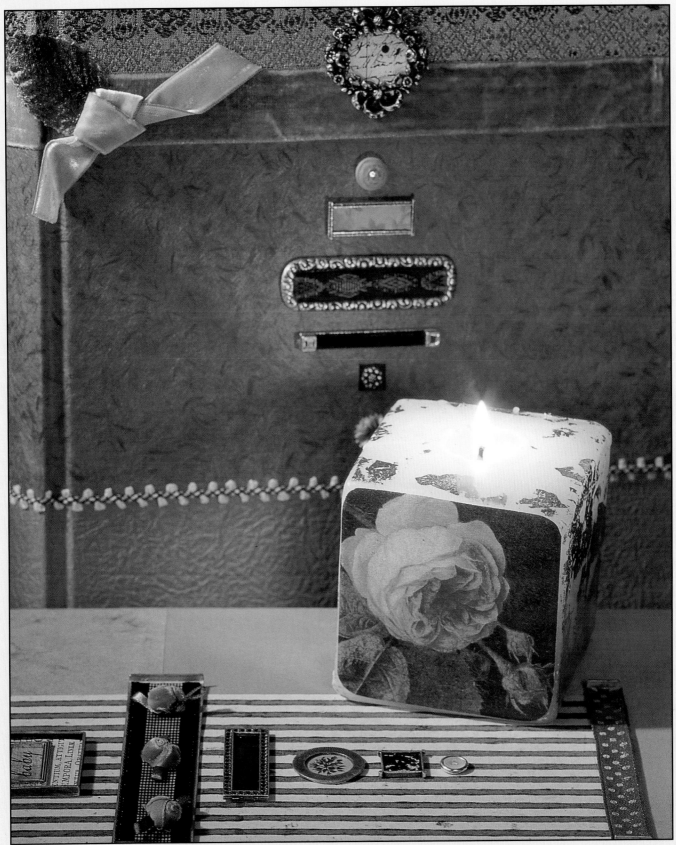

16
project

What You Need to Get Started:

Candle thermometer
Dipping vat: deep enough to accommodate enough wax to submerge candle
Double boiler
Glue pen with sponge applicator
Multiple-wick candle: cream
Paraffin wax (½ lb)
Pressed flowers

Pressed flowers can turn a plain candle into an eyecatching decoration. This multiple-wick candle was decorated by gluing pressed flowers onto the candle, then dipping it into melted wax to seal. This method can be applied to any smooth-surfaced candle.

Pressed-flower Candle

Here's How:

1. Prepare work space. Refer to How do I prepare my work space? on page 22

2. Melt wax in double boiler until it reaches 180°F. Refer to How do I melt wax? on page 16. Proceed with Steps 3–5 while wax is melting.

3. Prepare dipping vat. Refer to Project 15, Step 4 on page 80.

4. Arrange pressed flowers on candle as desired.

5. Using glue pen, apply glue to back of pressed flowers. Adhere pressed flowers to candle. *Note: Pressed flowers can be carefully repositioned if glue is still wet.*

6. Pour melted wax into dipping vat 1" depth over mark on vat.

7. Holding onto wicks of candle, dip entire candle into melted wax in one smooth motion. Remove and place candle on waxed paper.

8. Press down any flowers or leaves that protrude through the wax.

9. Allow wax to set.

Pressed-flower Candle Tip:
Pressed-flower candles can be made even more attractive by scenting the wax to complement the flowers used.

17
project

What You Need to Get Started:

Candle: mauve, oval-shaped
Candle paint: metallic gold
Foam plate
Natural sponge
Water

How do I sponge paint onto a candle?

Sponging is an effective way to soften the look of a dark candle or provide textural interest to a plain candle. This mauve-colored candle has been sponged with metallic gold candle paint. A heart charm has been attached to the wick, adding an unique touch to this handmade candle.

Sponge-painted Candle

Here's How:
1. Pour a quarter-sized amount of paint on foam plate.

2. Dampen sponge with water.

3. Dip sponge in paint. Sponge on candle as desired. Repeat until candle is covered.

4. Allow paint to dry.

Sponge-painted Candle Tip:
The candles shown at the right were done using the same candle painting method as the Sponge-painted Candle featured on page 85. Notice how the type and color of candles used create completely different looks.

18 project

What You Need to Get Started:

Candle paints:
  burgundy;
  cream; lt. green;
  med. green;
  silver; lt. yellow
Foam plate
Paintbrushes: #4
  flat; #1 liner
Tapered candle:
  lavender

How do I decorate a candle with paint?

Painting is an excellent way to decorate your candle because of the smooth canvas provided. This lavender candle was painted with simple yet beautiful flowers. Follow the painting diagrams provided or create your own meadow of flowers.

Painted Candle

Here's How:

1. Pour a quarter-sized amount of silver paint on foam plate.

2. Dip finger in paint and rub randomly over candle.

3. Repeat Steps 1–2 using burgundy paint and overlapping part of silver paint.

4. Load flat paintbrush with cream paint. Paint flower petals on candle as desired.

5

4

5. Load liner with lt. yellow paint. Paint oval in center of petals for flower center.

6. Load flat paintbrush with burgundy paint. Shade behind flower center.

6

7. Load half of flat paintbrush edge with lt. green paint. Load other half with med. green paint. Stroke brush on plate to soften colors. Paint leaves on candle.

8. Load liner with med. green paint. Paint a vein in each leaf. Allow to dry.

19
project

**What You Need
to Get Started:**

Bamboo: thin
   garden cane
Cutting board
Hacksaw: small
Pillar candle
Spatula
Wax glue

How do I embellish a candle with bamboo?

Candles can be embellished in many different ways and with many different materials. Use dried botanicals that will complement your home's décor. The bamboo on this candle was adhered with a wax glue specifically designed for use with wax.

Bamboo Candle

Here's How:

1. Measure bamboo against height of candle. *Note: The bamboo lengths must be the same height as the candle sides.*

2. Using hacksaw, cut bamboo to measured length on cutting board. Cut halfway through each side and snap the cane across the cuts. *Note: Use this length of bamboo to measure the the remaining lengths.* Cut enough bamboo to go around the candle.

3. Using spatula, apply wax glue to one side of bamboo length and press onto candle, making certain it is straight. *Note: Do not allow bamboo to extend past base of candle or the candle will not stand straight.*

4. Repeat Step 3 for remaining bamboo lengths, placing side by side and avoiding any large gaps.

Bamboo Candle Tip:
Try other various dried botanicals to embellish your candle. Cinnamon sticks, twigs, dried apple slices, leaves, and dried chilies can be used in place of the bamboo. Make certain to use a complementary colored and scented candle.

A doubled length of raffia can be wrapped around adhered botanicals and tied in a double knot. Ends should be trimmed as desired.

20 project

What You Need to Get Started:

Animal-print fabric: sheer
Craft scissors
Decoupage medium: gloss
Pillar candle: tan sandalwood
Sponge brush
Waxed paper

How do I decoupage fabric onto a candle?

Decoupage is the craft of applying decorative paper or fabric onto an object and sealing them in place. Decoupage a single candle or several, mixing and matching different jungle-print fabrics and candle shapes as featured below and on the facing page.

Jungle Candle

Here's How:
1. Cover workspace with waxed paper.

2. Cut fabric to height of candle plus ⅟₁₆", by circumference of candle plus ½".

3. Using sponge brush, apply decoupage medium onto candle.

4. Apply cut fabric to candle, allowing fabric edges to overlap at sides. Smooth with fingers to remove creases and bubbles.

5. Allow to dry until tacky.

6. Apply several coats of decoupage medium over fabric. Allow to dry between coats.

7. Trim excess fabric from top and bottom of candle.

21
project

What You Need to Get Started:

Candle dye chip:
  dk. brown
Candle paint:
  dk. brown
Candle
  thermometer
Dipping vat: deep
  enough to
  accommodate
  enough wax to
  submerge candle
Double boiler
Foam plate
Freezer
Metal spoon
Nylon stocking:
  soft
Paper towels
Permanent marker
Pillar candle:
  square, tan
Sponge brush
Taper-blend par-
  affin wax (1 lb)
Water

How do I give my candle a cracked appearance?

A candle can be given a cracked appearance by a method called overdipping. Cracking of the top layer is done by placing the overdipped candle in the freezer. When an overdipped candle is cracked, it reveals the candle's true color underneath. The candle featured on the facing page shows light-colored cracks against the dark-colored candle for a dramatic look.

Cracked Candle

Here's How:

1. Place candle in freezer for two hours.

2. Prepare work space. Refer to How do I prepare my work space? on page 22.

3. Melt wax in double boiler until it reaches 180°F. Refer to How do I melt wax? on page 16. Proceed with Steps 4–5 while wax is melting.

4. Pour two quarter-sized amounts of dk. brown paint on foam plate.

5. Dip sponge in paint. Sponge on candle. Repeat until candle is covered. Allow candle to dry for a few minutes and, while paint is still tacky, place in freezer on waxed paper for 20 minutes.

6. Dye wax. Refer to Technique 2, Step 5 on page 30.

7. Prepare dipping vat. Refer to Project 15, Step 4 on page 80.

8. Holding onto wick of candle, dip entire candle into melted wax in one smooth motion. Repeat dipping two additional times. Remove and place candle on waxed paper.

9. Place candle in freezer for two hours. *Note: The longer the candle is left in freezer, the more cracks will appear.*

10. Allow candle to come to room temperature. Using fingers, carefully press the outside of the candle to smooth out any air bubbles.

11. Using nylon stocking, buff candle for a smooth, shiny finish.

What You Need to Get Started:

Candle with 3" or longer wick
Embellishments as desired

How do I embellish wicks?

Embellish a wick by simply attaching a treasure or trinket onto the end. Embellished wicks add a special touch to the unique candles that you have created. Embellish a candle wick with something that makes a statement about yourself or the candle that you have created, making something commonplace look extraordinary.

Embellished Wicks

Here's How:
1. Embellish wicks as desired.

2. Make certain to remove embellishments and trim wick to ¼" before burning.

Embellished Wicks Tips:
The purpose for making a fancy wick is to add a little something special when the candle you are making is to be a gift. Design the wick to complement the candle—if there are seashells in the wax, you can drill tiny holes in miniature shells and string them from the wick's end. Try using an assortment of beads, buttons, or pieces of vintage broken jewelry. Embellish the wick by braiding it with embroidery floss, speciality yarns or threads, or thin ribbon.

You never know when a new idea for wick decorating will appear, so make the wicks longer than necessary—they can always be trimmed if you choose to keep the candle rather than giving it as a gift.

Section 4: *decorating with candles*

Collecting and theme decorating are becoming increasingly popular and both are easily accomplished with candles, candleholders, and minor accessory pieces. Here an outdoor garden party at the base of the rocky mountains has a "down by the seashore" theme. The candleholders are actually flowerpots that were purchased at a discount store. They were filled with sand, adding not only ambience but stability to the white pillar candles. Seashells that were collected on a vacation to the beach have been drilled with tiny holes, strung with ribbon, and hung on the table's edge. Easy, inexpensive, and yet the perfect solution to unusual decorating needs.

Candles can be displayed in so many ways. The candles featured on this page and the facing page show the endless possibilities of decorating with candles in any room. From aluminum pipe holders to martini glass holders, let your creativity blossom. Or simply place your favorite Tracie Porter® candle into a treasured fabric candle ring like the one below from Whimble Designs®.

Artists today are creating candles and candleholders of every style and design. The candleholders featured on the right and facing page were purchased in several different handmade-gift shops and show the possibilities for turning almost anything into a candleholder. One shown hanging on the facing page is holding a shot glass, one is a vintage glass lamp shade, and others are ordinary votive holders that are wired and beaded for hanging.

From this inspiration, try taking everyday objects and filling them with candles. Some suggestions might be: wine glasses, vintage canning jars, teacups, an assortment of vases, small discarded trophies, or whatever else sparks your imagination. Make certain that there is enough of an opening for the candle to burn properly and that the container will not become overheated while the candle burns.

Floating candles can add radiance and romance to any background. When displaying floating candles, do not waste the space beneath. Fresh or silk flowers, marbles, glass shards, or even glass trinkets can be placed in the water below the candle for a unique presentation. One of the glass cylinders contains a fully bloomed begonia, and the other, a glass frog. Use a memento or keepsake to design a one-of-a-kind display.

Metric equivalency chart

mm-millimetres cm-centimetres
inches to millimetres and centimetres

inches	mm	cm	inches	cm	inches	cm
⅛	3	0.3	9	22.9	30	76.2
¼	6	0.6	10	25.4	31	78.7
⅜	10	1.0	11	27.9	32	81.3
½	13	1.3	12	30.5	33	83.8
⅝	16	1.6	13	33.0	34	86.4
¾	19	1.9	14	35.6	35	88.9
⅞	22	2.2	15	38.1	36	91.4
1	25	2.5	16	40.6	37	94.0
1¼	32	3.2	17	43.2	38	96.5
1½	38	3.8	18	45.7	39	99.1
1¾	44	4.4	19	48.3	40	101.6
2	51	5.1	20	50.8	41	104.1
2½	64	6.4	21	53.3	42	106.7
3	76	7.6	22	55.9	43	109.2
3½	89	8.9	23	58.4	44	111.8
4	102	10.2	24	61.0	45	114.3
4½	114	11.4	25	63.5	46	116.8
5	127	12.7	26	66.0	47	119.4
6	152	15.2	27	68.6	48	121.9
7	178	17.8	28	71.1	49	124.5
8	203	20.3	29	73.7	50	127.0

yards to metres

yards	metres	yards	metres	yards	metres	yards	metres	yards	metres
⅛	0.11	2⅛	1.94	4⅛	3.77	6⅛	5.60	8⅛	7.43
¼	0.23	2¼	2.06	4¼	3.89	6¼	5.72	8¼	7.54
⅜	0.34	2⅜	2.17	4⅜	4.00	6⅜	5.83	8⅜	7.66
½	0.46	2½	2.29	4½	4.11	6½	5.94	8½	7.77
⅝	0.57	2⅝	2.40	4⅝	4.23	6⅝	6.06	8⅝	7.89
¾	0.69	2¾	2.51	4¾	4.34	6¾	6.17	8¾	8.00
⅞	0.80	2⅞	2.63	4⅞	4.46	6⅞	6.29	8⅞	8.12
1	0.91	3	2.74	5	4.57	7	6.40	9	8.23
1⅛	1.03	3⅛	2.86	5⅛	4.69	7⅛	6.52	9⅛	8.34
1¼	1.14	3¼	2.97	5¼	4.80	7¼	6.63	9¼	8.46
1⅜	1.26	3⅜	3.09	5⅜	4.91	7⅜	6.74	9⅜	8.57
1½	1.37	3½	3.20	5½	5.03	7½	6.86	9½	8.69
1⅝	1.49	3⅝	3.31	5⅝	5.14	7⅝	6.97	9⅝	8.80
1¾	1.60	3¾	3.43	5¾	5.26	7¾	7.09	9¾	8.92
1⅞	1.71	3⅞	3.54	5⅞	5.37	7⅞	7.20	9⅞	9.03

Index